This Book Belongs To

_____

_____

_____

Copyright © 2020 by
Color BD Publication

All rights reserved. No part of this publication may be reproduced, distributed, or transmitted in any form or by any means, including photocopying, recording, or other electronic or mechanical methods, without the prior written permission of the publisher, except in the case of brief quotations embodied in critical reviews and certain other noncommercial uses permitted by copyright law.

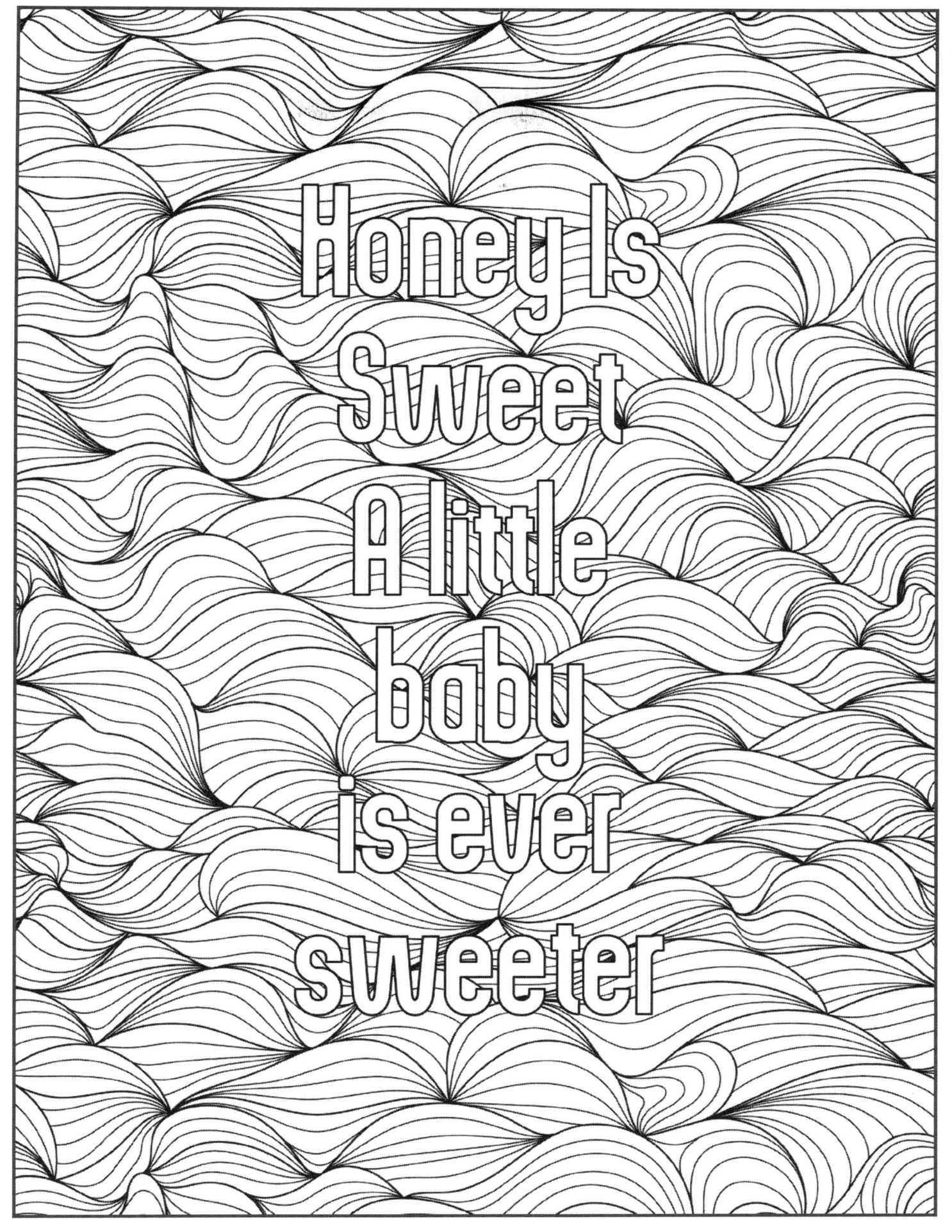

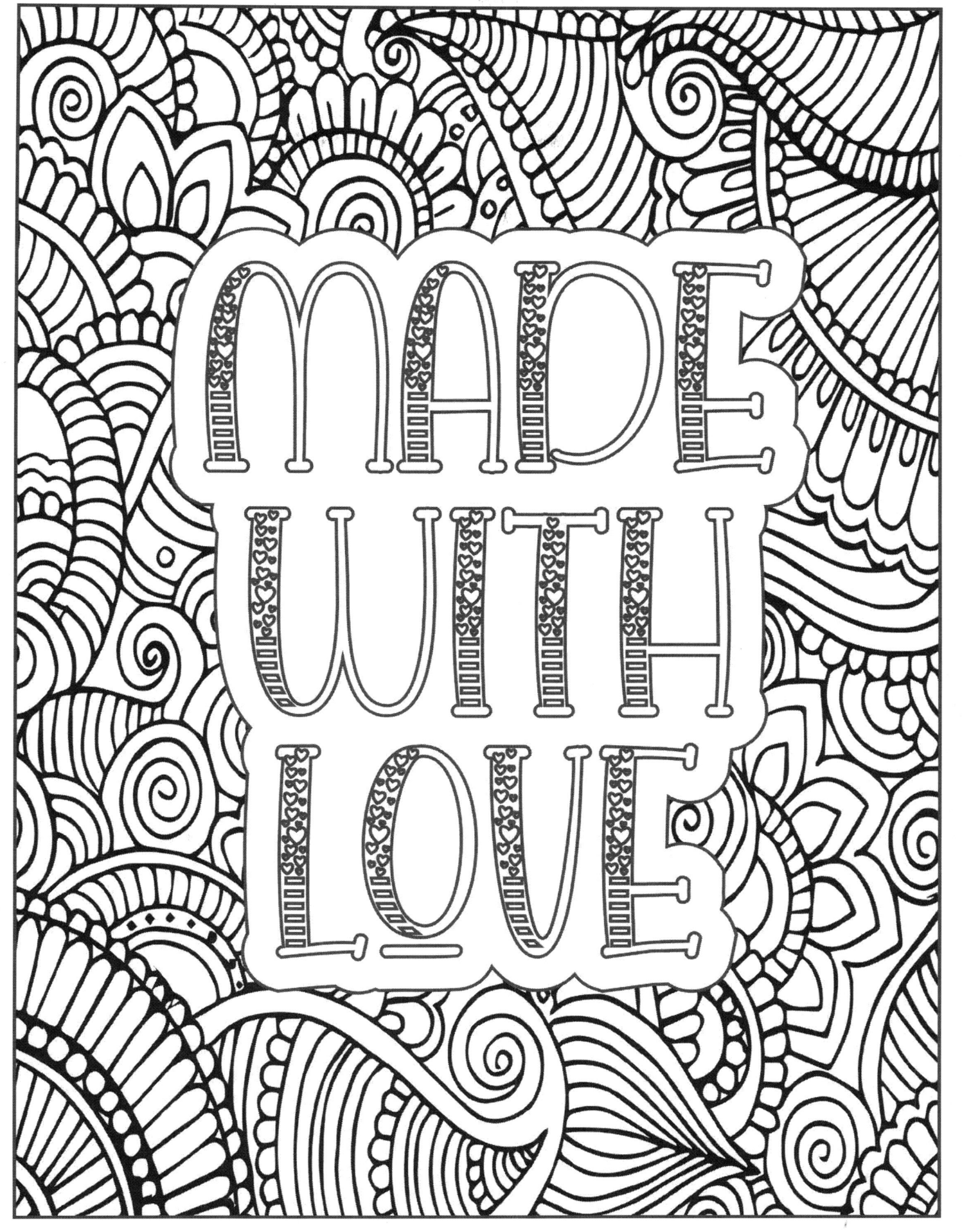

NAPS & BABY KICKS PREGNANTLIFE

Baby ....loading

DADDY'S BOY MOMMY'S WORLD

This Is Why, This Is Why, This Is Why I'm Hot

NINE MONTHS IN MY BELLY AND A LIFETIME IN MY HEART

ALWAYS BELIEVE THAT SOMETHING WONDERFUL IS ABOUT TO HAPPEN

BRA OFF
HAIR UP
BELLY OUT

The Baby Made Me Eat it

A Dream come True

I WILL MEET MY BABY TODAY

I AM BUILT FOR BIRTH

I am Built For Birth

Today WILL BE A Good Day

You Are My SUNSHINE!

GOD KNEW MY HEART NEEDED YOU

Happiness Is Carrying A Whole World Inside You

SUPER TIRED

SUPER HUNGRY

SUPER PREGNANT

TODAY IS going TO BE GREAT DAY

Printed in Great Britain
by Amazon